WHAT DO YOU DO
WHEN THE WHOLE APPLE
OF YOUR MARRIAGE
BECOMES
HALVED?

WHAT DO YOU DO
WHEN THE WHOLE APPLE
OF YOUR MARRIAGE
BECOMES
HALVED?

COLETTE ADESUA NEMEDIA-KUPONIYI

authorHOUSE®

AuthorHouse™
1663 Liberty Drive
Bloomington, IN 47403
www.authorhouse.com
Phone: 1-800-839-8640

Published by AuthorHouse   04/28/2012

ISBN: 978-1-4678-8909-4 (sc)
ISBN: 978-1-4678-8910-0 (e)

Any people depicted in stock imagery provided by Thinkstock are models, and such images are being used for illustrative purposes only. Certain stock imagery © Thinkstock.

This book is printed on acid-free paper.

Because of the dynamic nature of the Internet, any web addresses or links contained in this book may have changed since publication and may no longer be valid. The views expressed in this work are solely those of the author and do not necessarily reflect the views of the publisher, and the publisher hereby disclaims any responsibility for them.

CONTENTS

DEDICATION

MY SWEET DEDICATION WILL GO
TO THE CHILDREN OF GOD ALL
OVER THE WORLD WHO WILL
NOT ALLOW ANYTHING STOP
THEM FROM REACHING THEIR
GOD AND THEIR MAKER.

ACKNOWLEDGEMENTS

APOSTLES, PROPHETS, EVANGELISTS,
TEACHERS, PASTORS, BISHOPS ETC

INTRODUCTION

Tossing and turning like chicken being grilled or roasted. The pain unbearable. Your bed feels like its on fire. All of a sudden, it has become too big for you alone because your spouse that is supposed to be with you is no longer there. Your eyes become so wide awake because you are fighting sleep and cannot even sleep. There is no difference between yourself and the owl because you are up all night and the owl is also awake. Everything pales into insignificance. No longer conscious of time because it seems like even time has stopped in this new and grim world that you have now found yourself. Thinking, is this my lot? You can hardly smell coffee not to mention tasting it. Your whole body feels numb and out of use. You walk around your house which was home like a zombie trying to figure or make sense of it all. You look to the ground trying to find answers or solution as to what occured and how it can be resolved but can't find it anywhere. You cry every chance you get like its the IN-THING. Call everyone you know hoping that one of them might have just the answers you are looking for and all you get back from them even compounds your heartaches because like the discovery channel you discover all the thoughts that were hidden in their hearts concerning you and your spouse. You have your diary beside you like the yellow pages. You beat the carpet asking God why? why? why? and all you get back is great silence, not great calm which would have been a lot more soothing than the absolute silence. I felt God was not there. I even felt as though he was getting entertained by it all which I did not find funny at all. I told him often that if He was laughing, I certainly was not. I asked Him to kill me many times and that I did not write an application to be born. Since He was refusing to do His job of correcting all that had gone wrong. I told him that I did not want to be here and that He should take me and take me fast. At the same time I couldn't bare the thought of losing my children. You stop cleaning the house because you do not see the importance anymore. You cannot even dress up because all your bones are aching and you do not even see the use or point. You even forget to feed the children because you are in a limb state. My three year old started fending for himself when I was no longer attending to his needs. I'll often find him at the foot of the fridge eating raw okra and licking butter because he is hungry and I'll break down in tears because I cannot explain the reason why things have deteriorated. My confidence sky rocketed to zero. I was wearing shame as a designer label and garment. My baby just use to help himself to his bottle which was my breast at the time whether I was up to it or not. He knew where to find it—just underneath my blouse / t-shirt. Even though I was no longer feeding properly because of loss of appetite. Somehow the baby found a reason to suck. I guess it had become his dummy (pacifier) as well. My three year old suffered all sorts of verbal and physical abuse in my hand which was unnecessary because of my frustration. Jeremiah 33 vs 3 which was God's direct number was there all of the time. Which is what I should have called from the beginning was just lying there in the pages of the bible. God was right there even though I did not feel His presence. He certainly heard me everytime I called. He answered me. Yes He answered me. He gave me the life of His Son Jesus. He made me to understand that I am not only a conqueror but that I am more than a conqueror through and in His Son Jesus. The devil is a l-i-a-r-r and may he forever be frustrated with his agents and cohorts in Jesus Name Amen. My ministry is to frustrate him always. Amen.

You lose interest in bath time. The only time water comes in contact with your body is when you are running the tap over your head because of the constant migraine. My house and all the rooms became as the continents of the world that you do not visit. Everything and everyone suddenly looked strange because of a missing factor or should I say Key. You become a stranger in your own home because every other room represents some strange country. eg I became isolated by the enemy to my bedroom which represented Nigeria (home) A familiar territory. The living room became France, the dinning room Romania, children's room became China etc. etc. I could no longer tell which category I was in whether male or female because all the features in my body had shrunk frightenly. I had permanent stress lines on my forehead whether asleep or awake. You could write a letter on my forehead, the only thing was that you could not post it.

CHAPTER 1

WHEN YOU ARE MARRIED BY NAME ALONE

Your spouse even though gone physically, his memories are still very much with you to date. Even though he has left you or has been forced and pressured to leave you to devastate and destroy you, his name is still on you like a second skin. You have his name like a permanent tatoo on all your documents such as your passport, statements of account, account name and details, on every important document that you own and have.

The name is not only on paper, it is also on your lips, your mouth and the mouth of others. You are asked your name and the first and truest thing that comes out is the Mrs so so so and so that you are and bear. The case is all the same with those that know you as well as officials and staff that call you from banks, schools and councils etc. whenever I heard the name being called and of me being addressed as Mrs . . . the pain came flooding back. All I could think was, if only they knew where he was and all that was happening. By this time, it was beginning to dawn on me that I had been left and forsaken though hard to come to terms with. You do not sleep when you do not see your loved ones. My spouse could unless he had been sedated by someone or something consciously or unconsciously, he could sleep through it all because he had not contacted us and did not seem like he'd ever contact us even though I kept all of my hopes displayed, afloat and alive.

Mrs was written all over me. All those I came across that didn't know me knew that I had a man. A Mr somewhere but weren't sure if he was at work or on holiday. I honestly thought that his going would most probably be like a sabatical after a year of not seeing or hearing from him. Unfortunately, I realised it was more than that even after waiting for him for nine years and hoping for a reconciliation before the divorce documents were delivered through the post like any other mail.

I called his and their 'bluff' by signing the divorce papers in annoyance, realising from the documented evidence that I had not been his prayer point. Divorce came and went and still the name Mrs, hung on me like a door knob, a poster and a bell. It just will not leave me even though I really and sincerely wanted to leave it behind somewhere. Even when I refused to fill my forms stating

MRS, people will not just stop refering to me as Mrs Colette Kuponiyi. You can run but you can't hide. I just simply felt and thought Mr isn't having this problem for sure. He was Mr before I married him and he is still Mr after the divorce. Whom do you SUE in all of this?

CHAPTER 2

WHEN THE WHOLE APPLE OF YOUR MARRIAGE BECOMES HALVED

WHEN THE WHOLE apple of your marriage becomes halved other things get halved too. Your dignity gets halved. Your social circle and status gets halved. Your finances and fancies gets halved. Your friends and visitors get halved. Your image and importance get halved. Your worth and value gets halved. Your exuberance gets halved. Your wardrobe gets halved because his things are gone including the ones you use to wear together to match which you can no longer wear. All these inadequacies and ill appearances of no longer measuring up or up to standard was only in the eyes of people that know and use to know you. It was certainly and definitely not so with God your maker and creator. You were still very much valued and precious in His sight and He was more determined to pull and bring out those hidden treasures that the enemy had sat upon for ages that he did not want to manifest in your life.

God's operation started where man threw in the towel. The hardest part of all of this was having to explain to your very young children who could never in their formative years comprehend all that was going on or the degree of emotional damage that was still to come. It felt like their daddy had just gone to work or was on a long haul travel that was making him see less and less of them. It did not stop my three year old from always standing on the sofa by the window and checking if the car that just pulled up was his dad's or someone else. As many cars that pulled up by the house was as many times that he ran up unto the sofa, stand at the window, pulled the curtains to see if that was his daddy. Unfortunately, it was never his daddy. You can imagine what his thought must have been and the disappointment that he had felt time and time again.

The days to come after that at his school were also pretty much the same. My three year old's work was affected in every way. He could no longer draw a complete picture in art lessons of his family. He had a bad reaction one day at school that set the alarm bells ringing. I was called into school that there was a state of emergency with my son and that I should turn up as soon as possible. I did all I could to get there as fast as I could only to be told that he was having a bad day at school and the teacher demanded to know all that was going on at home. I was forced to tell them everything and explain to them how we were trying to patch things together in the mean time. The main trouble was that an assignment to draw a picture of their complete family had been given of mum, dad, brothers and sisters if at all they had any. My son proceeded to draw his family but put dad in a far corner of the picture and then scribbled all over it with black crayon which caused a concern to all of his teachers on that day.

As I examined the drawing, tears welled up in my eyes as I could only imagine what he was experiencing but I was so glad that they called me and got me informed and involved. It was one of the blackest days of my life with many more to follow. Even though physical death hadn't occured but something special seemed to have died in our lives that was causing wrenching and unbearable pain.

CHAPTER 3

WHEN THOSE VACUUMS
BECOME TOO MANY HOLES

W HEN YOUR BODY and your heart is constantly
experiencing pain and you pray for relief and
release from the pain you are experiencing but do not
get it, you feel like a super-spicy peppered chicken
externally and internally. You feel as though you drank
acid or something like it. The pain in your heart is so
huge that if you could get in there, you'd treat it with
every medication you can get hold of and finally plaster
and bandage it and wait for the healing process to reach
completion of pain all-clear and gone now'. In my case,
none of the healing was taking place. It seemed like the
pain was always doing multiplications in my heart. It was
wild, cruel and crude. I found it hard to concentrate on
anything serious for long. I needed a divine intervention
at an accelerated speed if there was such a thing.

Remember, I felt God was not there. How could He, if He was allowing everything I thought was in-human, unfair, despicable, unjustified, wicked and evil to be happening in my life. Not to mention in the lives of my babies. I felt, surely He can't be there. He's even extended it to the children, oh how abnormal it is, for a God that is suppose to be good, merciful, just, true, powerful and mighty to just sit up in heaven with His arms folded and do absolutely nothing. He couldn't possibly care I thought. What a nasty set up. I had started to bleed from every pore because even the One (my maker) that I had expected to intervene on my behalf did absolutely nothing. This made the vacuum of my life end up as many holes that nothing could fill or correct. I felt physically, emotionally, socially, spiritually, psychologically depleted in every way. I needed God's strength and power to get me through each day. I saw myself as alone in this world.

The lives of other people seemed to be moving and going on whilst mine seemed to have stopped. Everything everywhere with me was turning upside down fast and spiralling into impossible control. I had no control over any thing. As a result I got into a totally hopeless state wishing that I could just sleep and not wake up. Wishing I could just appear before my maker. I wanted God to beam me up but He just refused to do that which I was asking and pleading with Him to do. I felt utterly and totally drained, tired and knackered. I began to age faster than a ferrari at full speed. All I could see in the mirror was this ugly duckling. It was like my real face had been stolen and replaced with another from out of this world. My body looked like it had been exchanged and sold or given to someone else and I thought, wait a minute WHO AM I?

What clothes no matter how beautiful can one possibly wear on a broken down and defeated body? What smile could I possibly plaster on a face that was no longer mine? Who in the world could I be relevant to now, in such a state that I was in? What good I thought to myself would I possibly be interested in or want to have? I just wanted to go back to my maker, wherever it is that I had originated from. It seemed like my exit will do it and nail to the coffin the horrible and reproachful experiences. The thought only came about as a result of the vast vacuum in my life and all that was going on. All of it had came from the pit of hell.

CHAPTER 4

HOW TO TURN THOSE DARK CLOUDS INTO CLOUDS OF GLORY

I MADE A CHOICE that I wasn't going to sink. It was either I believed God. held His hand, sought His face and direction and allowed Him to lead me wherever He wanted to lead me. I began to find every reason to go to the assembly of God's people like I had never done before. I needed to hear His word, know it and apply it to my life. I never missed any meetings or services and I was always the last to leave the church premises. The only time I went home was when I was reminded to go because they wanted to lock-up. I needed God like I had never needed Him before simply for my well being so that I could in return be there for my children. I went home after church and switched on the christian radio for the second part of my upliftment. I found great pleasure in worship and praise which became like therapy for me. I found myself getting succour from His presence. Things were getting off-loaded from off of me as I worshipped and praised my Father in Heaven.

Not only did my confidence get boosted, my strength multiplied and I soared like I had never imagined was possible spiritually and it was evident physically. I could do and achieve things much more easily. God gave me clear direction and enabled and empowered me to carry out divine tasks and instructions. For once in my life, I started hearing God and knowing exactly what He wanted and would have me do. No matter how little, trivial or insignificant it appeared or seemed.

Worship became a drug for me. Much more like my best or favourite food. I couldn't get through the day without rendering to God His due benevolence of worship. I was so consumed with the worship of my maker that it didn't matter where I was. I would look for a secluded corner and when it was hard to find one, I'd worship anywhere with my hands lifted up. At the bus stop, in the car park, on the lift, in the bus, along the road, in the shops, at a restaurant, whether alone or with people. I would find a way of communicating my love, affection, adoration, praise and gratitude to my Father by simply acknowledging Him with a wave, a quiet praise with words, a dance move, an applaud or just simply by standing to pause, all in awe of this great God and majestic King of the entire universe. The One that fashioned me in my mother's womb. The One that nothing can compete with. The One that holds me in surrender all the time. the One that makes me wonder and question why He loves me so much. The One that is always there when no one else is. The One that continually makes a way where there seems to be no way. The One that never allows my foot to be moved. The One that restores me and mends all of my broken wings and bones. The One that is a shield, a shelter and a buckler. The One that quenches all the fiery darts of the enemy and brings all of their wicked devices to absolutely nought. The One that is the lifter-up of my head. The One that beautifies my life and satisfies my soul and my lips with goodness and good things. The One that crowns my head with Glory.

Who is like unto this Our God? Who? In his presence, there is fullness of joy and at His right hand are pleasures forevermore. I saw depression give way in His presence. I saw lack of confidence give way to total confidence. I saw lack flee from His presence whilst favour took its position. I saw my deserts giving out and giving off water. Giving became a norm in His presence. I was lifted in His presence. I accomplished things so easily with His hand in my hand. I had a new lease for life as opposed to before when I did not want to live. I became gradually equipped in His presence. I could tell the enemy to shut up in His presence. I discovered whom I was in His presence. Glory to God Almighty.

CHAPTER 5

HOW TO TURN YOUR PIT
INTO A PALACE OF PRAISE

M Y HOUSE WAS like a dungeon, unkept and it forbade the invasion of visitors who in my mind were only coming to spy and laugh at my predicament SO I kept them at bay. How? By not answering the door whenever they came. I made sure all my curtains were drawn with no sign of life in the house. We would try to be as quiet as a mouse and stay in the back rooms watching t.v or something so that no one would suspect my being there. It was easy to think that we had been deported or exiled by the way the house appeared from the outside as though no one had lived there in twenty odd years.

It was my brainer. An idea to get people off my case with their numerous interviews and questions about whether he called me, saw me or the children, phoned us, sent us money to feed etc. I had been there, done that and had a big and bold T-shirt to advertise it. It was now getting stale. I was trying to find myself and my life by getting hooked up with God, my manufacturer and my navigator. I needed to be alone with Him alone to teach me and show me where I missed it. I needed to know my commissions and omissions and how I could be better as a human being. I wanted to be His child again. All others had forsaken me. Even if I hadn't been His child or favourite, I needed to be just that now.

The praise and worship of Him landed me just where I wanted to be—on His very lap, not even at His feet which was where I had started form initially. From resenting and rejecting Him to seeking Him with all of my heart. My alabasta box needed to be broken and poured out at His feet even though it wasn't much. I wasn't going to let Him go. I needed Him for dear life. I wasn't going to expire and die before my time. How could I? I was only just getting to know Him and reverencing Him. Surely, I needed more time to show Him that I was His child and that He hadn't created an error by forming me. I needed him to know that I was very useful to Him and His Kingdom. His help was all I needed and I was determined to break down any door to reach Him as He had reached out to me. He was mine now. The bond had to grow stronger with each passing day and I was ready. Ready to do all that was required to develop our relationship.

I started to enlarge my heart to accommodate Him. All
the things that had been enthroned that were contrary
had to be dethroned. I needed God to have the very top
most and first place in my life. He alone was worthy.
Him alone deserved my praise and undivided attention.
Nothing else would satisfy or make me content like my
God and maker. He was the source of my life and I was
clinging unto Him for dear life after all. What else could
possibly matter, apart from this mission to get, grab and
grow in God? The most honourable way I discovered was
to enter into His courts with intensifying praise. A praise
that registered in the Heavens. A praise that came from
the depth of my heart. A praise that was undiluted and
unpolluted with self and ill motives. A selfless praise. I got
so lost in praising and worshiping the God of the heavens
and the earth which in return translated me into His
marvelous light where all sorrow, sickness and shame was
utterly snuffed out of my existence. A place where fresh
life was given to me. A place where I fully connected to
who I was in Christ Jesus. A place of victory and exploits
in God. It was a place self-less service to God where I just
wanted to do good as Jesus did and nothing else. In this
place, my desire for kingdom matters and affairs were
fully fuelled by the God of creation, The Holy Spirit and
Jesus The Son of God. In this place, my triune being was
made completely WHOLE.

CHAPTER 6

GYMING AND JAMMING IN GOD

M Y WORKOUTS WERE in God. Like-wise my dancing
and rejoicing was in God. I developed spiritual
tissues and muscles from these spiritual workouts. I would
worship Him for hours on end until I did not have any
clothes on except for my pant and bra as I would work
out a sweat. I just did not want to stop honouring him
in that way. He deserved all of my praise for keeping my
sanity and preserving my life that I had wanted Him to
take from me in my ignorance and also for restoring lost
hope to me.

I wasn't going to allow anyone or anything steal 'His'
time from me. I had to give him all that I could render
in worship and praise and it had to be digestable and
palatable to Him. It simply had to be the best. All or
nothing.

My workouts were always in God, which I reference as gym or gyming in God. They were physical, mental and spiritual workouts. I did loads of meditation of Him and His word which I still do constantly in between any activity that I do. The other thing I did was jam in God. All my social endeavours and activities were always centred around God and all that He represented.

My dancing, rocking, singing and jamming was in God. I sought for ways to please God in everything that I was involved in whether people liked it or not. As far as I was concerned, it was between myself and my God and no one else.

I noticed that the more I did these Godly pursuits, the more light and free I became. I became more friendly, more peaceable, more joyful, more forgiving and understanding and even more beautiful. Nothing of the enemy could hang around me for too long. Negative things were dropping off of their own accord and many victories were borne as a result of my hobby and pastime. Time belonged to God and I was determined that He would have most of it if not all of it. His reigns were on me as a result of my heart cry for Him and God Almighty continued to meet me at every point of need. I lacked nothing and wanted for nothing. The things He did not allow me have were for a a very good reason. The things He wanted me to have, I had in abundance. My supplies were regular and never late. I became empowered as He continued to satisfy my tongue and mouth with good things. My life became the life of God because I was now empowered and enriched by His unfailing and undying love.

The Bible says, let every man be a liar and let God be true. God became so true and so real to me that nothing could bring doubt or change my mind about His love towards me The scripture that says God will never leave not forsake us became all real to me. This in essence gave me the essentials to love as God loves, give as God gives, be real as God is real, be kind as God is kind, be true as God is true, be open as God is open, be helpful as God is helpful, be accommodating as God is accommodating and so on and so forth. I became translated and transported from one level of glory to another. Promotions came about as a result in spiritual, physical and material ways. I did not have physical cash like David Beckham but out of my belly flowed great rivers of great living water.

This was my Natwest and Barclays bank. With this kind of flow anything was possible. Just as no one can measure God's worth in monetary terms SO it is with His children. Our monetary value can never be measured or accounted for because we are like the oceans that never run dry because we are self producing and because Our Father has over loaded us with goodies. Amen!

CHAPTER 7

FROM THE PIT TO THE PALACE

THE PRAISE, WORSHIP, honour and adoration of Him, telling Him the right words and letting Him know my worries and cares catapulted me from the pit of the enemy into the palace of His very presence. His presence came down to me in the most tangible way that I could feel and touch it. WOW! It wasn't for an hour or a day, it became normal in my life to carry and have his presence with me. It was more than life itself. It made me ooze with confidence and believe that I could do and conquer anything that was thrown at me. I was no longer a victim but a victor that was victorious in every way.

I arose and stepped up higher in my walk and work with Him. The praise of Him enabled me to appreciate praise-worthy things. It brought out the best in life and living thereby giving me a sense of purpose and direction. There wasn't anything to make me wonder about my reason for being on earth or for been created.

Life had a lot of meaning and I could not wait for every assignment God had for me to fulfill and accomplish. I was content within myself and wanted for nothing. I had no reason to be like the Jones'. As a matter of fact I felt that the Jones' could take a cue from my life and the light of God in me. I was as joyful as I could be and I could shrug out any situation that wanted to get me down, depressed and dejected. I always entered into His gates with thanksgiving and into His courts with praise. This in return, mirrored the real person that I was to me. A queen. Afterall, this is how God sees His children as princes and princesses, Kings and Queens. I was able to love myself more as I discovered how much God loved me and in return I could love others genuinely with no contrary agendas and motives. The worship and constant worship of God gave me self worth. As I released myself unto God in worship, my Father in return released Himself unto me in a warm embrace. I was affirmed in His presence and reminded that I was loved regardless of everything going on around me. I felt whole and complete in worship and extremely powerful and fearless. My God's size and enormity became reinforced. He was indeed bigger than what people or I say about Him. It was hard for me to conceive that such a big God will shield and surround little me with all of His love. I could sense and feel all of His love encompassing me from the crown of my head to the soles of my feet. Nothing could beat or even compete with this experience. An experience that took me from the darkest valley and pit to the highest mountain and palace.

The adoration of God enabled me to adore others. I could see God in people of different races, tribes and tongues. Looking at people made me appreciate the hand work of God as a creator. My achievement of this was because of the reverencial fear of God that was in me. I am still praying for the fear of God to dominate my life because the fear of the Lord is the beginning of Godly wisdom. This fear helped me to respect God, honour Him, acknowledge Him and enthrone Him. It enabled me to treat others as I would like to be treated. It helped me to put God in His rightful place on the throne of my heart.

When you are able to discover the palace of your life in God, material things become of less importance to you. I say, whoever has God has everything including provision, protection, peace, love, joy, gladness, contentment, satisfaction, hope, faith and a lot more. These things are of by far greater value than the troubles around us. God gives peace even in the midst of storms. He has a way of reassuring you deep down that everything will be alright. He can be humourous at times, when He says something funny to your Spirit and you laugh uncontrollably. If God can make you laugh whilst you are crying or anxious about something, it simply means heaven has sorted it.

CHAPTER 8

FINDING FULFILLMENT IN PURPOSE AND SERVING

THE VOIDS IN our lives can be filled by all sorts. They can be filled with good things, bad things and even ugly things. I found a beautiful and wonderful thing to fill all the voids and vacuums in my life. this great thing was found in Christ Jesus. The Lord and saviour that died for the sins of the world simply to reconcile man to God. John 3:16 of the Bible, the living Word of God says that ' For God so loved the world that He gave His only begotten Son that whosoever shall believe in Him shall not perish but have everlasting life'.

The only way to reciprocate the love that Christ had shown to me on the cross was to serve Him in His Kingdom and embrace all of His purposes for my life. I could not find anything more refreshing, satisfying, comforting and fulfilling than serving in the house of God on every level and with all capacity that was within me.

I served with a heart of gratitude. I made my availability known to my Pastors and fellow workers. Nothing was above or beneath me when it came to serving. It was and its still a great joy to serve. It did not matter if it was serving an individual or serving corporately and generally. My service to the Lord and the things of the Lord developed a strong and healthy stature in my spiritual walk with the Lord. The evidence could be seen in my growth, development and fruitfulness. God showed and continued to show Himself mighty on my behalf. I was able to find my true identity in Christ, love myself as well as love others. Serving in the house of God lifted off yokes and burdens from my life. The favor of God rested on me. I found myself doing and accomplishing stuff that were totally impossible for me to accomplish before. My family saw me as super man or should I say super woman. They wanted to know my other secrets apart from the obvious. There were no other secrets apart from having Jesus Christ in my life. He was the secret and my only secret. A secret I was willing to share with anybody and everybody. As I embarked on cleaning the toilets at church gladly and properly, God Himself started cleaning up my entire life by beautifying me in my situation. There was no way you could see me and believe that I had the know how of cleaning loos and toilet floors. It was great fun and I always looked forward to doing it. I also became an usher and a greeter.

The amount of testimonies I received during the time of rendering this service in the house of God was uncountable as well as mind boggling and mind blowing. It wasn't long before I became ordained as a church deacon. Who was I to turn down the promotion and elevation of the Lord. I had to accept whole heartedly with no special airs and graces only plain and sincere gratitude. I was indeed grateful. I may not have been where I wanted to be or had all that I wanted to have but I was no longer where I use to be. There was no feeling sorry for myself. Rather, I was more interested in others and what they were experiencing in their lives. I was willing to be there for those that I could be there for. The Lord had comforted me and I was equipped to comfort others with all of the comfort He was giving me. I was practically eating from the palm of the Lord. He was meeting and supplying all of my needs and giving me even those things that I did not ask for. I found it very difficult to fathom His love for me.

His love towards me brought me to tears all of the time. At times, the tears of joy were uncontrollable especially when I look back at the hurdles, the valleys and the mountains that He helped me overcome. In whatever situation, I found myself in, I was more than confident that the God that did it before will continue to do it again and again. Somehow His joy was always inside me and this in return produced strength in me.

CHAPTER 9

HOW TO TURN THOSE DARK SEASONS INTO SEASONS OF HIGH PRAISE (POWERFUL, REFORMATIVE AND INNOVATIVE SEASONS OF EXALTATION PAR EXCELLENCE)

DARK SEASONS MEAN great reasons to upgrade the praise of Him that called you out of darkness into His marvelous light. When you do not see light around you, it means there is an absence of it and the easiest way to call it forth is by intensifying your praise because when the praises go up, the glory comes down. Even when sin has caused darkness to come, take it to God in prayer, confess and repent. Remove the brakes from your praise vehicle or vessel which is yourself and your mouth and take it above the standard limit by upgrading and increasing the authenticity of your worship. Let Him have it non stop. When you are down, it means it is time to take up your praise to Him. He inhabits the praises of His people by coming to live inside it and if God is living inside your praise, it means the aliens and the strangers will have to vacate your premises without being informed. When the King arrives, every nonsense must cease. They may observe you but they can't touch you in His awesome presence. God also helped me to see Him in all things. I could appreciate the hand work of God in all things visible as well as invisible. The greatness of God was re-emphasised by His creation. The beauty of His people, plants, flowers, the sun, the rain, the moon etc. This beauty could be seen in His attributes such as His enduring goodness, faithfulness, mercies and compassion.

All this appreciation and gratitude towards God stirred up great praise, worship and adoration inside me. When all of it was too much for words, I would lift my hands up to Him in surrender with a sincere heart of thanksgiving. There were often numerous times when the Spirit of God in me would reject the praise and thanksgiving because it was lame and wasn't accompanied with dance. I began to dance and rejoice before God like it was an addiction and a drug that I could not live without. Every time, I came into His presence in this determined and I-mean-business way, yokes would be destroyed and sorrow, sickness and sadness would have to take their exit because it was obvious that there was no lurking and hiding place for them to stay. In fact, their death and burial took place every time as I embarked on this ministry of praise and worship to my God, The King of Kings and The Lord of Lords.

My dark seasons would come at different times. These seasons could be as a result of family news that was not pleasant or domestic issues that want to cause panic and stress. Letters that threaten and bills that want to deny you of sleep but I could overcome them all when I stepped into the glorious presence of God through my exalting and exhorting of His name and His word. All the cases and accusations the enemy had against me, were trashed and thrown out in His presence.

Wisdom, knowledge and understanding starred me in the face in His awesome presence. Solutions poured out to me from simply entreating The King with my praise. I always made sure that my worship was not diluted, carnal or fake. My worship was with intensity and had direction. The direction was to God and for God alone. I could confidently say that my praise and worship was acceptable because it was from the depth of my heart and soul.

He was my priority and He was number one in my heart. The throne of my heart was fully occupied by Him.

Everything else could occupy the back seat of my heart but not my God. The maker, genesis and revelation of my existence. My Alfa and my Omega. My beginning and my end.

THE END . . .